NONSTOP
LOVE LIVE AND GIVE
My Angel, my Must, my Hero

JEN VUHUONG

Copyright @ 2015 by Jen Vuhuong

(3rd edition: 2017)

Dedicated

To my younger sister, Quynh, I would like to say, "We lost you so early. But we have lived for you, and believe you went to another better life."

To my eldest sister, Lan, who is my ANGEL, I would like to say, "Without you, I would be like a tree without water. Without you, I would be like a kite without a string. Without you, I would not be who I want to be."

To my other elder sister, Toi, who is my MUST, I would like to say, "Without you, I would be like a wing without power. Without you, I would be like a kite without wind. Without you, I would not be who I must be."

To my elder brother, Tien, who is my HERO, I would like to say, "Without you, I would be like a hero losing his strength. Without you, I would be like a kite without a good flyer. Without you, I would not be a hero within myself."

And to my parents, who brought me to this world, giving me my ANGEL, my MUST and my HERO, I would like to say, "Thank you"

Thank for inspiring me to be "***Non-stop living, loving and giving***" every moment of life!

I love you all.

Note to my amazing readers

I am just a person who is dying to share with the entire world how grateful and beholden she is to her sisters and brother who have saved her life, have always loved her unconditionally, intensively and have given her all the best things.

This entire book is all about that. It is completely based on my own memories, memories I have had since I was a kid. Seeing all the struggles of my siblings - almost dying, dropping out of school, choosing their own life route, standing on their own feet since their early ages, sacrificing for my family, courageously overcoming difficulties - I have been inspired to be non-stop living meaningfully, purposefully and vibrantly, loving completely and openly, and giving devotedly to make a difference for myself, my family and people around me. They are my ANGEL, my MUST, and my HERO. My love for them is unconditional, overwhelming, and knows no bounds.

To my amazing audience who are reading this book, I feel honored that our paths have crossed and that I have been able to share with you what I have learned from my amazing siblings. I strongly believe you are here because deep within you; there is a restless stirring to ***non-stop living meaningfully, purposefully and vibrantly, loving openly and completely, and giving devotedly***. I believe this desire will increase, as you read this book.

From the bottom of my heart, I would like to express my thanks to you. I believe you are all awesome and I would love to have an opportunity to listen to your stories one day! I hope our paths cross again someday and I will be able to share with you my upcoming books belong to the same series about ***Non-stop living, loving and giving***. Until then, let's be together non-stop living, loving and giving every moment of life!

Contents

Dedicated 3

Note to my amazing readers 4

Contents 5

The yellow smiley kite 9

My ANGEL 10

   3 years old, Recognising my angel 10

   11 years old - Winter Blanket 10

   12 years old – Cycling and ice cream 11

   12 years old, Heartfelt birthday gift 13

   13 years old, The Pikachu shirt 14

   18 years old - The entrance to the new world 15

   The pigeon guy – My unexpected brother-in-law 17

   My expected brother-in-law 19

   Now, Two people instead of one 21

   The day I left… 22

   The reason for living 23

   Every day till Forever. 24

My MUST 25

   A risky card chosen 25

   A risky card given 26

   Energy colour and the cost of my momentum 27

   The fighting of being happy single 30

   The right one 32

   Wedding day, tears to actions 33

   I was the reason 35

My HERO 38

   The first golden ticket 38

   The second golden ticket 40

   My brother-made childhood 41

      Summer time 41

      Autumn time 41

>>Spring time 42
>>Winter time 42
> My brother-made adulthood 43
>>First route chosen 43
>>Risky route given 43
> My brother-made student life 44
> My-made brother girlfriend 46
> New Hesman 46

What is the thing you feel most thankful for in life? 47

Gratitude moments 49

About the Author 51

"It makes you feel alive. It makes you thrive.
It makes you cry. It makes you feel like you can fly.
It makes you excited to wake up every day.
It makes you take action to better yourself in every way.
It makes you live to honour struggles. It make you live to love others. It makes you live to give.
It has you living meaningfully, loving openly, and giving joyfully every MOMENT of your life — nonstop.
It is your purpose for living."

Today I am inviting you to make a decision to be nonstop loving, living and giving every moment of life.

_Jen, your friend, performance and leadership coach and trainer
Jenvuhuong.com

"I fall in love with the world every day... What I mean is I fall in love with people: how they think, how they express themselves, their courage in chasing their dreams, their commitment for family, their spirit, their integrity demonstrated each day as they face a sometimes difficult world, their laughter and their striving and their hope and empathy. I love people as my brothers and sisters and mentors and friends, as kindred souls living joyfully and dutifully under this big canopy of Grace."

_ Brendon Burchard

The yellow smiley kite

On a windy sunny day

"Look at the sky - there is a smiley yellow kite flying. How can it look so energetic and excited like a human being?" People are excited.

On a foggy day

"Look at the sky - this smiley kite is flying higher. How can it fly in this condition?" People are surprised.

On a freezing day

"Look at the sky - the smiley kite is getting even higher. How can it survive in this condition happily?" People admire it.

On a stormy day

"Look at the sky - the smiley kite is flying in a love heart shape." Instead of asking HOW, people start smiling with the kite.

My ANGEL

I woke up after staying one week in hospital after a serious accident in which I had lost a litre of blood. My mind was foggy and I could not see anything clearly, but I saw someone removing the shells from some shrimps and feeding me. I saw that person, that angel, who told me: "It will be OK. You will get better soon. I love you." Every day, I would see that person taking the shell off each shrimp, feeding me, and falling asleep with exhaustion. One month later, I had recovered my strength, and could run and play with the other kids again. That person saved me. That person had brought me back from the edge of death. That person I recognised as my angel: my sister.

3 years old, Recognising my angel

At that time, I was 3 years old, and my angel always seems to remain as young as she was the first time I recognised her. She has an oval loveable face with kissable cheeks that she inherited from my mother. You will always see a smile on her face. Her smile is not only bright like the sunshine, but also charming with an irregular tooth and full lips. Her eyes radiate pure love, honesty and care. She easily gets worried because she is so thoughtful that she thinks about all the potential situations and consequences that could happen, which even makes her angry sometimes. However, she never takes more than a minute to control her anger and start taking the best action to make sure everything is going well with everyone. She is a very organised person who is always very demanding about the tidiness of the house, more than anyone else. She is a courageous woman who can overcome any difficulties to live, to love, and to give all the best things to people around her. **Her appearance makes people fall in love with her at first sight, and her personality makes people stay in love with her forever.**

At that time, my parents were staying in the hospital to take care of my younger sister, Quynh, who passed away a few weeks later. As the eldest sister, Lan had to take care of the house and three siblings, including me. She would get up early everyday to go to the market, and try to earn enough money to buy expensive nutritious food for us. How could a little 10-year-old girl take responsibility as a mum, as a dad, and as a sister? The only answer is love. Love is a choice. My sister chose to live to love and love to give her siblings all the best. She chose to be my angel to save my life, to love me unconditionally until she leaves the planet.

11 years old - Winter Blanket

I was a naughty kid. I always wanted to be the right one in any situation, so I would argue with my angel all the time. I didn't want to grow up till the day my angel moved to another city to study. For the four years my angel was away from home studying, I wished I could have taken back all the naughty words I had said to her. I changed, in order not to be as stubborn as a mule. I grew up. I appreciated each and every moment we spent together when she came home to visit. I became her good listener and advisor. She would always tell me about all the things that had happened in her student life in the big city in a positive way. She opened up a new vista with all joyful and amazing experiences so that I could be more motivated to willingly engage in that environment. I had never clearly imagined the difficulties she had in her student life as she never divulged any information in that respect. I sometimes wondered how she could survive on only 25USD each month from my parents, but I never seriously asked her about that.

One day, while we were planting rice seedlings together, we talked about how the winter was so cold, and I joked, "It seems that the winter there in the city with millions of people is not as cold as here."

"It is pretty cold, but my friends' kindness has warmed it up," she said. "Wow, such nice friends, I bet they love hugging you," I laughed. "They gave me a blanket", she said.

I felt bitter about how much she had struggled. I felt hurt. I realized I had never asked her about whether she could afford to buy jackets and a blanket for the winter with the little money my parents gave her. "What does she eat every day? What does she drink every day? How can she buy books for studying? How can she buy pens for writing? How can she be so positive?" Thousands of questions came to my mind that shut my mouth up and sent me into silent mode. I wanted to have a share of all the difficulties that she faced when she was living away from my family's home with such little supporting money. I knew that she would never have wanted me to worry about that. I knew that I could not help her financially in any way at that point, but I could give her moral support. I eventually changed into a cheerful kid because of her. It was all about making her smile.

I felt more deeply and clearly the troubles my sister had experienced during her student life when I became a student. All the words she told me and all the actions she took were the best evidence that she did not want me to have to experience all the difficult things she had faced as a student. **She laid a strong foundation for me to be ready to engage in life joyfully, courageously, positively, and meaningfully.** The first thing she bought for me when I moved to the city to study was a winter blanket. The blanket itself did not keep me warm in the cold weather and protect me from loneliness, but my sister's love did.

12 years old – Cycling and ice cream

The year 2000 saw one of the best memories in my entire life. I had been waiting for the summer holiday for my angel to come home. I wish I had hugged her, if only time could go back, to express my love and how much I was looking forward to seeing her. But, culturally, it would be extremely odd in Vietnam, especially in the countryside, to hug her to welcome her back home. She seemed to have had the same feeling as mine when she arrived at home and saw me at the gate waiting for her. She gave me a big smile and brushed my hair, saying "I'll take you to the capital, since you have studied really hard. It's my small gift for you!" "Wow, I can't hold that gift; it's not small at all," I quipped as usual.

I was over the moon when I dreamt about going to the capital where I could see buildings, famous people, large supermarkets, big malls, etc, - all the things that I had only seen on TV before.

But, at the same time, I was worried about how my sister could afford to take me there; my parents would never provide me with money for travel purposes.

My sister read my mind: "I know how, so don't worry." Pointing at a bicycle, she said: "This is our horse; the prince will take the princess on the back of this horse." I could not utter a single word, but my surprised face told her "Seriously, are you going to take me to the capital, which is 70km away from my hometown, on that bicycle?"

The bicycle was an old-style cruiser, one which needs to be pushed really hard to move. The bicycle should only be used for fun activities, such as taking wedding pictures, as people usually do. Nobody would use it for cycling, but my sister would.

I sat behind her skinny body, seeing how she craned her back to pedal the bike. I saw her sweat, I saw her smile. Sometimes she would look back with a joke: "You're still there, great. Make sure that you don't fall asleep then silently fall off onto the street, OK?"

That image has touched the very depth of my heart; it has been engraved in my mind ever since. If I ever need to relive my childhood, that image will be the one to help me get there. My sister's struggle instilled more inspiration and motivation in me to study hard to make her proud of me.

How could a small girl be so strong and cycle with her sister behind for 70km! The one and only answer is love. **Love is a choice. My sister chose to love me unconditionally; making me happy was her source of happiness. People can become stronger than they can imagine when they love someone and do things for their loved ones. When I grew up, whenever I came up against difficulties, the image of my sister craning to pedal the bike would flicker in front of my eyes as a solution.**

Luckily, a gust of wind came over and drove away the exhaustion of the heat. My heart was singing in harmony with the rhythm of the wind. I closed my eyes and smiled inside my heart, as my sister did, at the same time. I don't believe there is heaven, but if it does exist, that must have been the moment I was in it.

We arrived in Hanoi. In the eyes of a child born in the countryside like me, the city looked huge. Buildings were next to each other, and the noise of vehicles in the crowded capital created a really special feeling. This was the place where I would go to study soon. I definitely would do it, not only for myself, but for my sister.

We then headed straight to my sister's rented room. Everyone called my name and gave me a big smile as if they had known me for quite a long time. My sister used to tell them about me. I felt the love everywhere, love that was shared between my sister and her friends.

I had a great night's sleep after a long day of travel and walk around the big city. Although supposed to be the one feeling exhausted already, my sister, with a smiley excited face, said: "Let's go get some ice cream, sweetie!"

Although I wished very much to say "Great", the scary idea of wasting my sister's money made me hide my excitement, so I just said "OK", instead.

She read my mind again, "Don't worry, I have 30 cents. I've been collecting the unused papers and selling them. We can buy 3 ice creams, one for me and two for you." I cried inside as I thought about the financial difficulties my sister was facing, without knowing anyone, with just a little bit of supporting money from my parents. I saw how amazingly resilient and courageous she was during her 4-year study. I entered university, and tried not to take more than 40 USD per month as my sister did, no matter how many times my sister asked if I needed money. I went to work part-time, I appreciated each cent, I appreciated each page of white paper and I felt what my sister had felt.

That ice cream is probably the sweetest and bitterest one I had ever eaten in my life. It was full of love and effort by my sister to make me happy. Even though I tried to eat slowly, so as not to finish the first ice cream so that my sister would not need to buy the second one for me, my sister could read what I was thinking about and kept pushing me to finish the two ice creams, then most of the third one that she pretended that she could not finish.

Ice cream, the word itself and its taste, has since then served as a reminder for me to live meaningfully and purposefully to make my sister proud of me.

12 years old, Heartfelt birthday gift
Before the sunrise, my sister woke up early, as usual. She ran to my side: "How did you do that! Don't do it again, OK?"

"OK! I won't do it again, but I will do other things," I smiled roguishly.

I couldn't sleep the whole night before, and was so excited to see the results of my new invention: a heart I made from flowers for my sister's birthday. I had collected the small white flowers from a field nearby my family home the whole day before. I had secretly been plaiting the heart to surprise my sister. I smiled when I imagined my angel wearing a white dress, with the plaited white flower heart. I quietly put it beside my sister's bed when she was sleeping.

Her face radiated a smile which told me she was over the moon. However, she preferred to give me tough words so that I would not spend time and effort on such things again. To me, those words were sweeter than ever and motivated me to do more similar things for my angel.

Although people had told her to remove the old withered flower heart, my sister had kept it in her room till it was renovated for my brother to move in. She told people that the flowers had lived longer than usual without any withering because they were given from the heart.

Love makes a huge difference in everything we do and make. Whenever we put effort into making something for others, no matter what it is, they will love it.

I arrived in Paris, and took a bite of a Croissant and an Éclair. The heavenly, fabulous texture of the Croissant and Éclair reminded me of the best cake I have ever eaten: my sister's cake which she made with love and kindness. Whenever I went home, a plate full of cake was always waiting for me on the table. I would just automatically start eating non-stop as if I had been hungry for days. My sister's cake was simply made from flour, sugar and the most important ingredient: love. "Don't touch it, don't eat it. You only can eat it after the meal." She was really stern whenever she saw my hungry eyes fixed on the cake plate, since she knew I would skip my meal after eating the cake. As a cunning kid, I would ask her to look in the other direction and then quickly snatch a piece of the cake and run away to stuff it into my mouth and devour it.

I was so happy when I got the recipe from my sister. I loved making cake for my friends, when I stayed away from home, although I am not a good cook and I do not like to cook for myself. People started calling me a great cook and kept asking me about the secret. Nobody would ever completely believe that in fact the secret was LOVE.

13 years old, The Pikachu shirt
"Look at your niece, isn't she cute?" my sister asked, sending me an image. I could not move my fingers to type a single word, as I thought it was me. People would usually tell me that my niece was a copy of me when I was a kid. She was wearing a jumper, with a bright smile on her face, in the picture. It was my jumper. My sister still kept it, a Pikachu machine-knit jumper that she had bought for me when I was 13 years old.

That year, on 3rd April, I tried to guess what my gift was when I heard my sister's excited voice. I finally gave up the idea and asked her to just show me. She asked me to open my eyes to see the gift. I couldn't express how happy and surprised I was to see the Pikachu jumper. The Pikachu image in yellow was highlighted on a grey background. I have been nicknamed "Lovely Pikachu" since then. My sister had saved money for a whole year to buy that gift for me to make me feel like it was the very first time I had my own favourite winter jumper. I wore it most of the time, and it became part of my life. I grew up, and it became too short for me, but I considered it a new style. I didn't really know if I had loved Pikachu before or I loved it because of her since that day. With only this jumper, I could survive in any cold weather conditions, not because it was thick enough, but because of the warmth from my sister's love.

As I grew up, I could start giving back. I could do things for my sister as she had done for me. If before that I could only make everything by myself, I could now buy something and put my love into it for my sister.

She loved and appreciated every single thing that I gave her. I could not stop laughing at seeing my sister wearing the same clothes every time I went back home, even though the clothes became old and *soiled*. "Are you serious, aren't you miserable? Your house can't contain all clothes you own. Why do you wear the same old outfit all the time? You don't look nice in these clothes. Please wear the nicer ones and then I would love to see you more." She just smiled back, as usual. However, I was certain about the obvious answer, "I feel happy wearing the clothes you gave me, especially when you are with me." I could not utter a single word as I felt touched. One day I saw her heel scratched, and asked her which shoes had hurt her. "The shoes you gave me were tight but I loved wearing them." "What?" I was shocked and could not utter a single word as I felt touched.

Love is a choice. Love can make normal things special. Love can heal wounds.

18 years old - The entrance to the new world
In Vietnam, securing a place in a public university is considered a major step towards a successful career, especially for those from rural areas or disadvantaged families. This reveals a lot about Vietnamese society and its people. This mentality is prevalent particularly in my countryside, where education has enabled and empowered the youth to essentially choose their careers. University places are based on the scores achieved in the entrance examination. High school graduates need high scores to be admitted to university. The pressure on the candidates therefore remains very high, despite the measures taken to reduce the importance of these exams. Moreover, the exams are held in big cities only. Therefore, taking the children to sit the exam was always a big concern for any parents in the countryside, in terms of accommodation, food, and transportation in the city they have never been before. My

sister used to study in the capital, so she asked my parents to let her take me to attend the exam. It was a big event for my family. I knew that my parents believed in me, but they could not avoid being worried.

My parents had never had to remind me to study since I was 5 years old - the first time and also the last time I got punished because of not doing my homework. They believed in me. I was confident; I believed I could pass the exam to enter the university as a way of expressing my deep thanks, from the bottom of my heart, to my parents, and especially my angel.

"Don't tell me that you are going to take me on the bicycle and I will be the one to cycle," I joked, when my sister told me she would take me to the capital.

"We have upgraded to a motorbike now, the economy has developed, you know it," she said with a charming smile on her face.

My sister was like a Kindergarten teacher who took care of me, in terms of even the very little things. She brought as many things as possible, even a water bucket. In Vietnam, even in the big city, when you rent a student room, there is usually no sink or shower so you need to rent or buy buckets to contain the water to wash yourself. She took me behind, and the bucket was bouncing on the end of the motorbike. The sound of the bucket, when we went on the highway with its strong wind was uniquely memorable. I had a bad habit of always sleeping whenever I sat behind anyone. My sister with her skinny body was driving, worried that I would fall off. She would touch me sometimes tightly and keep reminding me "Hey, wake up. Are you still there?"

"Yes, I'm still here," I answered, with my eyes still closed. I would smile when I recalled the bicycle memory. "One day, it will be me who will take you by car or by plane. Wait for me," I reminded myself about the thing I that wanted to do for my sister.

People usually ask kids "How did the exam go?" even though they know that kids do not really want to talk about it; they just want to leave it aside. But my sister was different; she could usually read my mind. She would wait for me with a smiley face and candy in her hands every time I finished one subject. She knew I didn't like talking about things that passed and focused instead on taking action to move on. She tried to make me feel that it was great to finish one subject to move to the next one, until I finished the three subjects. I could see her worry, despite her belief in her independent little sister. I knew that one thing I could do for her was to stay strong, to stay positive. I did an even better thing for her when I took care of my brother-in-law's sister in the university entrance, as my sister did with me. **Sometimes, a simple way of giving back to your loved one is to be giving towards people around you.**

The pigeon guy – My unexpected brother-in-law

My sister went back to our hometown after graduating from university. One day she met a man in a photocopying shop, and that incident almost changed her entire life. The guy was a high ranking army officer. He fell in love with my sister at first sight, as most boys did. He started a flirting campaign to win her heart.

His campaign was based on a fight fast win fast rule; and he believed his wealth would be the key success factor. He built a bird house in my family's garden and bought a couple of pigeons as my sister loves this bird. He would come every night with lots of fruit and other delicious food. For the first time in my entire life I had innocently eaten the things that I liked everyday from a stranger. I hated the guy, but I did not hate the food. No matter how politely and kindly he treated me and my parents I hated him instinctively at first sight. My hatred towards him increased day by day as a natural process, but my love for his food did not decrease.

"What is wrong with you? How can you behave like that to him while you have been enjoying all the stuff he brings? Grow up," my mum complained to me.

"There is no problem with the food, mum. The fact that I love the food doesn't mean that I have to like the guy. He won't turn out to be a good man in the long run. That was my feeling when I first saw him. I can't stop my gut feeling. You will see soon," I confidently, sincerely responded.

My mum gave up the idea of changing my mind which she called *"the prejudice"*. She loved the politeness and thoughtfulness of the guy, as my dad did.

Since I was a child, I have always believed we need to give other people as well as ourselves a second chance to discover their and our beauty. Nonetheless, this belief was not working in the case of this guy. The first impression and the next time I met him just made me hate him more and more. After three months of the guy visiting our house, I put on weight - three kilograms - by eating his food.

I did not talk with him and ignored him whenever he stayed at our house. If I said something then, it was aimed at provoking him. As a small child, I thought "either him or me, only one of us could exist in this world with my angel." My gut feeling told me unconditionally that he was a bad guy for my angel- the one I loved most in my life, the one I could devote my entire life to. I did not want to hurt my angel, but I could not accept the guy, so I decided to keep silent as much as possible. I had a big internal conflict and a scary feeling that grew day by day when I saw my sister and the guy getting closer and closer.

But I had to break my silence on the day he proposed to my sister. My heart was swelling and beating fast. I found it hard to breathe, and I writhed in anguish. I ran away from home the moment I saw my sister was about to agree. As a kid, I felt I was going to lose my sister for a bad reason. I was going to lose my angel to a demon. My enemy, the demon in my point of view, won my sister's heart, so he won me. The game was over.

I could not do anything as I was just a little kid; my voice was not powerful enough to change the situation altogether. However, I could not accept the ugly truth. I wrote a letter and dropped it off at my sister's room: "I love you more than anything else. If you are going to get married to this guy, I am sorry I cannot be your sister anymore. I do not like this guy as I feel he is a dishonest person. He will not bring happiness to you in the long run. He just wants to own you."

Soon afterwards, I didn't know how I could have done that to my sister. She was really heartbroken with those superficial words. Written words may cause deep wounds to the people we love more than we could imagine. Written words, once delivered, cannot be taken back. My words left a deep scar on my sister's heart, one that could not heal.

During the following days we did not talk to each other. I knew my sister had been crying and had been extremely sad because of my letter. She did not say anything. I didn't know how I could open my mouth to talk to her again. I felt guilty and hurt, but I thought I would still have done the same thing, had the time gone back.

The man did not come to our house anymore. Two weeks later, my sister told us that she broke up with the man, to the surprise of my parents. I felt guilty when I felt happy at hearing that, as I imagined how really sad my sister felt.

After that day, I woke up, but could not hear the familiar sounds of the pigeons in the yard anymore. There were total 10 pigeons given birth by the original couple of pigeons brought by the guy. I ran right away to see the bird house and saw no pigeons at all, the bird house was empty. All the pigeons went away. It was certainly true that those animals stood for faithfulness, so when the guy left, they left too.

I felt a little bit of regret, but joked with my dad, "We should have eaten all of them before they left." My joke fell flat with everyone; it came at the wrong time.

Whether or not I was one of the reasons, I still believe till now that that was the right decision my sister made. Two months later, the man sent a wedding card to my family, to the surprise of my parents. He got married to another girl, right after breaking up with my sister.

I desired to talk with my angel and stay by her at that difficult time, but I did not dare.

Luckily, Sang came.

My expected brother-in-law

Sang, the most sincere guy I have ever met, loved my sister since the first year of high school, but he had never revealed it to anyone. My sister was unaware of the intensity of his feelings, and he was afraid of telling her out of fear of rejection. They held different spiritual beliefs and values. He never had to worry about earning money to support his study or his family, while my sister did. He was simple, while my sister was more complicated. He was very serious in pursuing a deeper relationship with her, as many other boys were. However, he just kept silent and followed my sister day by day. He felt sad whenever other boys approached her, but he then would remind himself that he would be happy as long as she was happy. They both went to the capital to study; he just kept following her in silence and was always there for her. **He was always there for her in her times of need, and he was there when she needed nothing at all.** He became known by my sister's housemates as an uninvited guest who would come every weekend.

Among all the men chasing my sister, I did not feel he was the most exceptional. However, he would be the most suitable one. My sister had lots of things on her mind, so it would be great, if she was with a simple guy, so that she could at least not feel more stressed. There is no doubt that "Diligence is the mother of good fortune". Sang remained beside my sister as one of the most patient people. People came in and went out of my sister's life, but he was always there for her.

Nevertheless, life always challenges people. My sister went back to our hometown after graduating from university, but Sang still had to study one more year. He managed to go back to the hometown to visit her every two weeks.

Unfortunately, the pigeon guy came into my sister life at that time. It was the most difficult time for my would-be brother-in-law when he saw my sister and the guy getting closer. He still kept silent, and just hoped that my sister would be happy. His sincere silence made me respect him, but at the same time I felt helpless.

Fortunately, an opportunity presented itself. One good turn deserves another. My sister split up with the pigeon guy. Sang immediately went back to console her. Naturally, he poured comfort into her heart as he had always done before.

Seeing his loved one feeling miserable pushed him to take one step further. At the very first opportunity, he spoke out and told her that he wanted to be the only man in her life.

Life still challenged the young sincere man, no matter how good his intention was. My parents began to really hate him, as he started coming to our house every day. My parents compared him to the pigeon guy in terms of maturity, thoughtfulness, behaviour, everything. To their mind, he was a kid, in comparison to the other man. They did not like him irrationally, as I did with the pigeon guy. I then told them they had *a "prejudice"* against one of the most honest men in the world. However, I could not change their minds about him.

For 1 year, whenever Sang came to our house, my parents would leave. He would still come, no matter how badly my parents treated him. Time passed, and my parents asked my sister and Sang about their relationship: "What is your relationship? How can a boy come to a girl's house everyday with no name for their relationship, Lan? There have been rumours and gossip about you guys."

To alleviate my parents' concern, Sang started calling them dad and mum. My father got even more angry, and wanted to kick him out of the house. He did not understand that my parents wanted him to bring his parents to meet them so that an official relationship could be established between the two families.

He finally understood my parents and had the courage to take the right action after some months. He brought his parents to our house, but a drama then started.

"I think they should not be together since both are of the same age. Lan will soon look older than Sang," his parents said brusquely.

My parents felt extremely humiliated by those words. My sister was a beautiful girl, and she always had boys around her that were waiting for her to say yes to their proposals. How could they underestimate my sister?

After that day, my parents told Sang that they did not expect to see him again. However, Sang still came to our house to see my sister every day. He kept coming to our house for three years. Everyone was wondering how he could be that thick-skinned to keep coming despite my parents' hostility. I myself still expected that he would become my brother-in-law eventually.

My parents were not as patient as Sang, so one day they told him, "If you do not give up, then we give up. We have to surrender to your patience and your sincerity. We would love to have a son-in-law like you. Why don't you guys get married?"

I learnt a great lesson from my would-be-brother-in-law, now my brother-in-law, about persistence and taking action. **When we have a goal, a burning desire, we need to take real actions, and if we keep working on it patiently and consistently we will achieve it and make people finally recognize our efforts.**

Now, Two people instead of one

In Vietnam around 10 years ago, the age of marriage may have ranged from 23 to 27 (except for 24 or 26 which are considered as unlucky ages for getting married) for people who went to university. These figures are lower in the countryside where people usually go to work early, and do not really pursue higher education. Couples usually live with the husband's parents, at least until children are born. The bride is expected to wait on her husband's family. Regarding the bride's family, when the daughter gets married, they do not expect she will have many chances to take care of them anymore. She would belong to the groom's family.

I did not think that traditional way, for I always believed that my sisters and brother, whether they got married or not, would still care about every member of my family. Nevertheless, I was also worried as my lovely sister would soon need to take responsibility as a wife in her own family. It meant that she would not spend as much time with me as before. It meant that our relationship would not be as passionate as before. I could not stop this stupid way of thinking, even though I knew for sure how much my sister loved me and that that love would never change, whether she got married or not.

The year 2007 saw the renewal and renovation of our family's house, all thanks to the hard work of my sister and her fiancé. For me it became a sign that I needed to be ready for the big event in my sister's life: getting married. I tried to calm myself down and allay my fear of losing my sister to my lovely enemy by keeping reminding myself how nice he had been to everyone in my family. I tried to control my heart by my spirit.

That day finally came. My sister did not inform me by phone about her wedding; she and the guy travelled 70km to tell me. "Why have you guys postponed it that long? You should have done that sooner. Look at you, 27 years old already, even though you look younger than that". I tried to joke with my sister although I wished she would have waited till I graduated as I would then be more ready for it. It was a shock for me that I thought would affect my study. On top of that, I had not done all the things I planned to do for her.

"And your family is not afraid my sister will get older than you soon, bro?" I tried to hide my emotional feelings by kidding with my future brother-in-law. As usual, he just kept smiling like a stone.

I invited my friends whom my sister had known since the first year I entered university to attend her wedding. I always wanted her to feel happy to be with people who loved her as I had done. I loved to see her happy to know that her love had been shared with all of my friends. If it had not been for her love, I would have not had much love to share with people around me. I felt it was my duty to spread her infinite love throughout the entire world. But

I must confess I would feel sad to think of the moment the guy would come to take my sister to his family's house. I could not stop that childish thinking.

Everything turned out to be totally opposite to the mentality of the Vietnamese people regarding marriage. My sister got married; my family then got taken care of by two people, instead of one. There was not even a small problem in my family that could be handled without the consideration of my sister and her husband. **I receive messages now, not from one person but from two. My angel got married. I have had an angel's assistant since then.**

The day I left…
I decided to leave Vietnam to start my own life and pursue my dream after working for two years for a foreign company which granted me a scholarship when I was a final year student. I called my sister and informed her on the day I was flying. I asked her if she had any big luggage bag or not, in which case I would buy one. I didn't really look forward to hearing the answer "yes" from her, I just asked her as I thought she would feel happy if she could prepare things with me before I left. She said yes and told me to just come home and take it. I was extremely surprised as I never thought she could have one, or at least the one that I was looking for. I thought she just wanted me to go home so she could see me. Nevertheless, I went home to visit my family, never expecting I would get the suitcase which stayed with me for 2 years (which for me is a long time) afterwards. It was a simple red suitcase that exactly matched my style. I wondered why she owned it, but rather than ask I just smiled happily and took it.

While I was staring at the case that I had never seen in my sister's house before, my three-year old niece said - "Do you like it? You know, I and my parents went to the city to buy it yesterday. I stood in front of the bike with the bag and held it. It was bigger than me."

"You bought it, why did you say you had it already," I screamed and then could not utter a single word. I wish I had not asked her. I should have expected this scenario because she had always done it before. "You are pregnant, 8 months pregnant. How could… It was…" I blamed myself. I felt ashamed to imagine my pregnant sister going all the way down to the city to buy the suitcase for me. However, I knew it was better to feel happy and take it, as usual. It was better for me to live more purposefully to make her proud of me.

Going to study in Europe with a full scholarship was a planned gift that I gave to my sister. She didn't say much, she never stopped me whenever I went anywhere, and she just said take care. She did not want to live away from me, but she loved to see me pursue my dream, my own life. I could see she was not ready to see me leave the country for a longer time than ever before, even though she had tried to live with that fact previously whenever I went on a business trip. She did not come to our family's house to see me; I knew she was scared to say goodbye. She did not call me as usual every day. She did not text me as usual every day.

"Where have you been? The princess is back in town." Finally, she called me three days before I left Vietnam. "Have you prepared everything? Have you documented everything and arranged it? This is a longer trip than others, so be careful." She did not say much as she knew I was independent enough to do those things but not careful enough to put things in order. *She was aware of my lack of carefulness more than me and anyone else. She always told me that if I was more careful, I could do everything in a much better way with less effort.* Two hours before the flight, I saw the 1st post on her Facebook profile that I had just created for her. "My sister has been a really important part of my life since I was a child. Today is a really special day, a day that I have expected and prepared myself for a long time, but I still want to cry. I have already cried thinking that I won't see my sister for a long time. My sister is going to a place far away to study. I remember every single day I saved my little money to buy the things that my sister likes. My sister is not at home anymore, I feel both sad and happy. I wish I could go back to my childhood." That was 28th August!

After reading the words from sister heart, I cried for the third time since I started being aware of things around me. I cried. I was overwhelmed by that big love. I had to translate it into real actions to make her proud of me.

The reason for living
"Do you really want me to die?" she said to me in a shaking voice. "You are so kind, so God won't let it happen. So, you have not eaten anything since you did not hear anything from me. I am so sorry, but you know your sister is so strong and is not that quick to die." I tried to reassure her.

"Don't say crazy things like that again. You didn't answer my messages. And I didn't know your new phone number. I couldn't contact anyone to ask about you. I just couldn't eat, drink…I just…Anyway, how are you? How is everything going? Have you eaten?"

"Hold on, don't tell me that you haven't eaten since the day I left. Aren't you afraid of looking older? Wrinkles will appear on your face and you will look bad, you don't want that, do you? Anyway, it's awesome here. Please go and eat something, otherwise I wouldn't talk to you anymore. You should have trusted your strong sister, as you have always done. I will take good care of myself, so please you do the same."

She then hung up and I knew she smiled inside and felt great when she heard my voice. I counted one, two, three, and she called again, after 3 seconds. "Have you eaten? Can you eat the food there? Watch out when you go out on the street. Do things carefully…"

"Yes, Madam. Keep smiling and stay beautiful and I'd then love to see you soon." I knew she would be happier than ever just by hearing my humourous way of talking to her as usual.

People need to breathe to be alive. People need to drink to be alive. People need to eat to be alive. My sister needs to know I am doing well to survive.

Every day till Forever…..

"Have you eaten? What are you doing? Take care! I love you." These words are sent to my phone everyday by my sister. I sometimes used to feel fed up reading the same messages every day. I told my sister I could help her to program it, so that it would automatically be sent to my phone every 24 hours. "That's different. When I type, with each word I transfer my love to you, which makes me feel alive and happy." I must confess I could not live happily without these daily heartfelt words.

I feel lucky and blessed to have my angel, my sister, in my life. Her love for me is so huge that I cannot return it in the same way, as she has done. I just know one thing I can do for her is to say "I am doing great. I love you." I just know one thing I can do for her which is to turn her unconditional love for me into actions, by non-stop living, loving and giving, as well as becoming the person I want to be and making her proud of me. I just know one thing I can do for her which is to think about her whenever I get lost in order to go back to the right track, stay focused and pursue my dream. I just know one thing I can do for her which is love, care about and motivate others, as she has done for me. I just know the best thing I can do for her which is to become an angel for someone, as she has been for me.

My MUST

Vietnamese people talk about the Heroic Mother as an honourable title for mothers who have made sacrifices for the construction of the nation. To me, my second sister, Toi is a Heroic Mother. She has sacrificed her life for my family since she was in her early years.

She has been a MUST for me to be the person I must be.

A risky card chosen

"Why do not you want to go to school? If you do not want to live the life of a farmer, the best way is to go to school." The tough words from my parents to my sister came when she told them that she wanted to drop out of high school. In a tougher tone, she said: "I hate school. Why do I need to go to school when I hate it?"

"You are such a naughty kid. You will regret dropping out of school" my parents gave up on her after telling her this unpleasant prediction. "I will not," my sister affirmed. One thing about my sister that everyone in my family, as well as the whole village, was aware of is that nobody could get her to change her mind as long as she had already made a decision. She was given the title the most *self-willed* kid in the village.

No matter how hard my father tried to convince her and told her about the consequences of the lack of education in the socialist society, she was "self-willed" enough not to change her mind. She hated school, not only because she could not grasp the full benefits of being at school, but also because she did not want to waste my parents' money. She would rather go to work to earn money directly.

In Vietnamese society at that time, and even now, dropping out of school would be considered a risky choice. My sister chose that risky card, despite the fact that everyone thought she would regret for the rest of her life.

Some months after choosing the "risky card", my sister was eager to say goodbye to my hometown to go to the South Vietnam, Ho Chi Minh City (my family is in the North, near the capital Hanoi).

I was really naughty and did not get on so well with her at that time, so I did not pay enough attention to remember the day she left our hometown. I heard that she was happy there since she could earn money and did not need to follow school disciplines. I did not have a lot of emotional feelings at that time, apart from thinking, "That is good for her."

As I grew up, I felt heartache when I thought about my sister's sacrifices for my family. If she had not done that, it would have been difficult for my parents to afford supporting me and my eldest sister in our study. On top of that, I learnt to *live independently and as courageously as she did.*

She worked really hard day by day, year by year. She recognised there was an urge inside her to go back to study. She registered with an evening school and worked during the day. She wanted to study again.

A risky card given
Sometimes, life challenges us. But challenges can be beautiful, if we see them as opportunities to discover our abilities and test our limitations. Sometimes life gives us a mystery card, which is either risky or promising, to open a new door to a new opportunity. My sister got that card.

On a rainy day, she was going back home from the class after two hours of study, with her smile radiating across each corner of the street. She heard some people screaming, "Get out of the way, a crazy motorbike is coming towards you."

She was not fast enough to move out of the way. She fell, with her entire leg covered in blood. She couldn't move her leg. It was pretty common for people in Vietnam to get drunk and still drive. No matter how careful you are, it is out of your control when meeting drunk drivers. It became a turning point in her life.

My sister was lucky to be alive, but she had to suffer throughout her entire life with the broken leg. However, this experience has made her get serious about doing things, including living more fully, vibrantly and meaningfully. She used it to lead a better life. The card turned out to be good for remarkable years of vibrancy, connection and meaning. This happens when willpower trumps brainpower.

My sister was lying on the road and could not move her leg. She felt stuck. Both bones of her left leg were broken. The drunk driver was scared and ran off.

My sister, instead of feeling hurt, was totally disappointed about life; why was she given that unlucky card which blew away her chosen card. She could not imagine how she would live her whole life with a broken leg.

The doctor said she would not walk as a normal person, no matter how much therapy she had undergone. The therapy needed some years. The image of a lady limping made her totally depressed.

In Vietnam, there is one thing about some doctors that I can never tolerate. When a doctor says IMPOSSIBLE, it means he or she needs more money. Money can increase the POSSIBILITY. However, in the case of my sister, even money could not help because the problem lay in the limitation of technology. I did not believe what the doctor said; I believed that when a person had a burning desire to live meaningfully, life would never give a card to kill the desire, but just to challenge it. We need to do whatever it takes then, we have no other choice, but to overcome it.

If the tragedy had not occurred, who would have known how courageous the small girl was. My sister finally got back to our hometown after the accident for which she was hospitalised for six months. She was dying to get back to work. She left our hometown again to go to a north-western city, 50km away. She was so passionate about becoming a cook, and there she found it. I heard that the owner of the restaurant loved her sincerely, and highly appreciated her hard work so she divulged her lifetime secrets as a cook to my sister. **The accident turned my sister's life into one of non-stop living, loving and giving.**

I entered university and the image of my sister with the broken leg made it imperative for me to take a real action to change it. I was searching for doctors at different famous hospitals, but I could not get a positive answer. But I never stopped hoping and believing. That image was, for me, a reason to live.

One day I read a shared experience of a speaker about some things everyone should absolutely do when living. One of the things was climbing a mountain. "So, what about my sister?" I asked myself. Every time I hiked, I was dying to have my sister do it. I would imagine my sister and I together hiking, climbing and jumping on the highest mountain in the world.

When we decide who we want to be, what we want to do, this eventually changes the way we do things. My relationship with my sister was in the best possible shape. Although we never talked about it, but my sister knew that her struggle in life was a motivation for me to rise up to the standard to do something for her. She knew that I felt I owed her my whole life. As for me, I knew that she tried to comfort me and show me that she was actually doing great and still keeping a positive attitude. She made me feel I needed to pay her back all that she had done for me in the form of an amazing life. She transferred to me the nice feeling of being loved and trusted and being hopeful. I felt I would do it for myself and for her. "I did not complete my study which would have opened a new window into a different world for me, so I believe you can do it perfectly for yourself and for me too," those words have been a constant incentive in my entire life.

Energy colour and the cost of my momentum
It was a day I felt lost and confused about what I had been doing in my life. I decided to cycle to Hai Duong, 70km away from Hanoi, where I was studying. To most Vietnamese people, it was a crazy thing to do - cycling alone 70km with a cruiser bicycle on a sunny day

on a Vietnamese highway without a cycling track in 37 degree-heat. I felt like doing it, so I just went for it. I craned my body to pedal the small bicycle; each tear that ran down on my cheeks reminded me about the day my eldest sister took me to the capital on a similar bicycle when I was 11 years old. ***I came to further appreciate the perseverance and stamina of my then small sister. That was the feeling I was looking for. I felt a little bit lost during that time; I had to get back on track. I needed a little PUSH.***

The hot weather could not keep me awake the whole way. I was pedaling and sleeping. I woke up each time I heard the sound of the horns of vehicles on the road or the shouting of people on motorbikes or car drivers.

The bicycle fell down and I ran away from it, not knowing what had happened, "Am I in heaven?" I was totally awake, I was totally intact. I just hit a car parked on the sidewalk. The accident I had when I was a little kid came back to my mind. I decided not to continue cycling until I was totally awake. I did not want to risk my life that way, I had to meet my sister who was waiting for me.

Finally, I arrived at my sister's place, safe and sound. Only when my sister came over and pulled my hands and dragged me to the kitchen to water and feed me, I knew that I was still alive.

"How was the cycling? You must be exhausted."

"Your sister is strong, you know that. That was great, I loved it."

I would never tell my sister that I was sleeping and hitting everything on the road, otherwise she would never stop worrying in the future whenever I cycled. My whole family would have called me afterwards to warn me not to do this again. The cold fresh water brought me back to the conversation with my sister.

"Wow, welcome. Thank goodness you arrived. Your sister has been crazily waiting for you. She was worried about you and couldn't do anything."

I was overwhelmed by the welcome of my sister's colleagues, and I knew that my sister was worried more than anyone could imagine. I felt the respect and kindness of people there towards the most sincere person in the world, my sister.

My sister took me to her room to take some rest. I almost could not hold my tears at seeing her living conditions, a tiny bed in a tiny dark dorm room. My inner strength made me hold back the tear and pushed me back to the point where I lost the route of my journey, the journey to live meaningfully and make a difference for my sister, for my family and for people around me. The girl standing just next to me devoted her life, and went through difficulties, to supporting her family financially and mentally. I owed her my whole life.

"People here are very nice. It is great to stay here. I actually just need a place to sleep. If I need to feel fresh, I just need to go to a restaurant hall or a garden, it is really fresh there, you know. I feel really comfortable here."

"Great", I responded briefly.

I knew that my sister tried to comfort me as she was aware that if she had to suffer anything, I would feel the suffering more than her.

That feeling has continued to live within me throughout my entire life. I felt the food I ate everyday and the clothes I wore everyday were made from her lumpy hands, wrinkled face and deep eyes.

She introduced me to all the people around her, and I felt how much she was proud of me. She then took me inside the kitchen and showed me the way she cooked chicken. She removed all the skin and feathers and sank it into hot water. I imagined her in a big kitchen in a white shirt as a chef, in a restaurant I was going to open for her. My life was motivated by the thinking of doing something that would help my sister do what she loved to do; cooking was the one thing that made her feel happy, as I could see. She asked the owner for a little time to take me out to the open market.

One day I looked at myself in the mirror and started feeling in love with myself in the colour yellow more than ever. I loved myself in the yellow shirt that I was wearing at that moment. I did not know since when I had loved yellow. Years later, I looked back and realised that that was the shirt bought by my sister. Eventually, yellow became one of my favourite colours for shirts. I felt energetic, hungry to live to love to give as my sister had done for me.

My sister asked me to buy everything I needed, while we were walking in the open market. To let her feel comfortable, I agreed to take the yellow shirt and refused to take any other things under the pretext that I could not carry them all the way back. I knew my sister knew that I did not want to waste her money. Empathy can connect people and they can then share the happiness and share the pain. I wish my sister had not put my happiness first, so that she would not have had to suffer.

I sometimes crazily thought that if I had a choice, I would choose to die before anyone else in my family as I would not bear the feeling of losing any of them. I would be like a table with broken legs and would not be stable. How could I be strong, if I was thinking this way, which indicates weakness and irresponsibility?

We walked on the way in the windy autumn with a little bit of sun shining on my sister's face. I imagined my sister and I were walking in paradise together, and I was keen to wait for her to choose her favourite clothes. As I was eager for success, I would sometimes fall in the trap of overusing those emotive images. I would become immersed in the fantasy and forget in the real world things take time and persistent effort.

Two days passed, I was about to go back to my studies. My sister pulled my hands, opened them and put 200, 000 VND (which was around 10USD at that time). "Just take that on the way back home." I took the money and saw the tears in it. **How much money do people need to pay to life coaches to gain momentum to live meaningfully, vibrantly, and happily to love unconditionally and to give devotedly? To me, the cost is 10USD.**

The fighting of being happy single
My sister sincerely made me both admire and worry for her. I was concerned that bad guys out there would easily take advantage of her. I would forgive everyone for everything, except for the ones who would hurt anyone in my family.

My sister came back to our hometown to work as a tailor for a factory near our house, as my parents expected. In Vietnam, especially in the countryside, people normally excessively care about what others say. My parents started reminding my sister day after day to get married when she turned 27. My parents had both internal and external motivations to keep telling her that it was so late for a girl to stay single till that old age. My sister's case was even more special, as they were aware that since she started working at the age of 16 she had never enjoyed hanging out with people or joining any social activity. To be honest, I was happy to see her single. My parents could not live with the rumour of my sister being given the title SPINSTER. In contrast, the childish thinking that "As long as my sister does not get married, I will have more time to spend with her" excited me to the point where I would always argue with my parents about the idea of being single and happy at the same time. My parents would sometimes feel so annoyed at me since my idea had a strong influence on my sister's decision about marriage. I knew that I had to grow up, I could not be so selfish to keep my sister beside me, and each individual needs a loved one. Instead of running away from the fact that my sister deserved a person to love her as much as she had done for people around her, I would rather let it happen. I changed the way I had talked about marriage in my conversation with my sister. I made her feel she should open her heart to the world to take any good opportunity coming into her life. **We all have abundant love, but if we keep the door of our heart closed, nobody can feel us and we can't feel love from others. Only when we are ready to receive and to give, can we see thousands of opportunities out there.**

I was ready to see that my sister could finally live for her own family. My sister changed her status from being a happy single to a person happily ready for marriage.

"Do you know that 'Cuong USD' is probably going to get married to Toi," my eldest sister Lan was excited to tell me on the phone. "Now I know it, you have just told me," I nodded. Even though I had said to myself I should be ready to hear such news anytime, I was still confused "Who is that guy? How is he? Is he the right one for my sister? And why so fast?" were questions that kept me awake thinking for days.

In Vietnam, there was a man called "Cuong USD", a nick name he has given as he had started wasting money in USD since he was a small child, while millions of other Vietnamese people in those days never even thought of having a USD to use in their entire lifetime. The way my eldest sister named the man created a strange feeling within me that something was going on there, that there was something wrong with the guy. Moreover, I never heard anything from my sister Toi, which meant that the guy was not important enough for her to be keen to introduce him to me. I arranged to go home to see what was going on there, as I would never let anyone make my sister miserable. I would even punish him for any hurt to my sister. She told me she did not like him. He was a total loser. He took her out and made her pay for everything. Furthermore, he apparently told her that she had to do all the work on the field as his family had 7 hectares of land and his mum was now unable to work.

"You don't need work on the field that much. You have worked for almost half of your life on the field; you do not need that anymore. Apparently, he is just looking for a person to take care of his land. You don't just like him because of his land, do you? We should simply tell our parents, and I am gonna kick the guy out," I said angrily.

"Our parents seem to know that, but you know they have waited for so long for anyone to propose to me."

"He proposed to you? How dare he? I will never let him do that to you. We have all the evidence to show that he is an asshole. I won't let him ruin your life. You deserve a much better person."

I was like a fierce tiger defending its cubs from getting hurt. I could see my sister did not like that guy's personality as well as the image he laid in front of her for the future. I talked with my parents to express my strong disagreement about that marriage.

"You don't want to ruin your lovely daughter's life for a farmer's life. We don't need that Cuong USD. We can find another Cuong Euro who is much better," I joked, but in a serious tone when talking with my parents.

I went back to the city for my studies, and could not stop thinking about the man and my sister.

The day I heard the news that the total loser - Cuong USD - was rejected by my parents and never appeared in my family's house anymore was a fabulous day for me. I jumped and screamed with joy which made my roommates think that I was drunk or crazy. Interestingly, the man was said to have got married to another girl just two months later. The history of my eldest sister seemed to have repeated itself with my second elder sister.

I came back home, and I felt I was actually the only one, apart from my sister, who was feeling happy after all. I sensed concern everywhere in the whole house. The happiness of getting rid of an asshole was not strong enough to allay the worry over the lateness in my sister's marriage. It seems I was the odd one in my family to always believe that being single is not a bad thing. I tried to get my sister to just enjoy being single and enjoy every moment of her life, and to love openly until the right one comes. I could feel my sister felt lost as to when the right one would come, given all that long time of wait.

The right one
But life is wonderful; everyone has a right match that just comes naturally. The right one for my sister came. I was not at home during that time, so I did not have many chances to meet the man till they informed my family that they could get married. Back then it was rare for a couple to move out of their parents' home before they got married. So, basically my sister and Truong never went out together at night, but it turned out they got married when she was pregnant.

I used to refer to my eldest sister's marriage as "slow food, slow marriage" and my second sister's marriage as "fast food, fast marriage". The slow marriage took 10 years, while the other took only 3 months.

Truong is a really good man; everyone who meets him feels that he would never ever hurt anyone, that he would never ever hurt even an insect. There is one thing in common between Truong and Toi: sincerity. **Sincerity begets sincerity, as per the law of attraction.**

The man, Truong, came to visit my cousin Tham, and planned to propose to her. But she didn't like him. Truong would come every day to Tham's house and try to find funny stories to make her feel happy. She seemed to have had no feeling for him. She just considered him like a guest whom she had to try to be polite to.

Truong would stay at Tham's house everyday till around 11pm, but Tham would also sometimes ignore him as she was so tired and wanted to sleep. Time passed and he met my sister one day when she went to visit Tham at her home. They started talking, and engaged in an in-depth conversation very quickly. Family and friends who saw them on that day were surprised that two people could build such rapport after only meeting once. After that meeting, Truong started visiting my sister. They chatted non-stop whenever they were together and always seemed to forget the time.

Valentine's Day came, and my sister was delighted when she saw Truong coming in with a flower.

"Can you help me with one thing?" Truong insisted sincerely.

"How can I help you?" my sister said, trembling with excitement. She thought it was a special way of proposing that he had planned.

"Get Tham to like me," the guy said innocently. Those words smashed my sister's hopes and her heart.

My sister could not say anything. She kept the sadness inside, and kept the conversation going with Truong. After that day, Truong went back to pursue Tham, despite the fact she didn't have any feelings for him. She treated him the same as usual - ignoring him. One week passed, and Truong went back to talk with my sister. Three months after he had met my sister, he went to meet my parents and asked for permission to marry her. My parents were both shocked and happy at the same time.

The wedding plans were proceeding so quickly that I did not even have enough time to arrange to go back home at the beginning of the preparations. My sister gave me a call to inform me about the wedding. "What should I do?"

Wedding day, tears to actions
I wanted to buy a wedding gift for her with my own money. I wanted to build a restaurant for her. I wanted to create a chance for her to do the thing she likes. I didn't want her to work as a tailor which wasn't her favourite job, but she just had to be able to afford her living expenses. I hadn't done anything for her yet. "What should I do?" I was tormented with the question.

I felt helpless to be unable to express my love for and gratitude to my sister - which is a common sense for me - in real actions. I knew clearly that my sister did not need any material wealth, but needed my love. However, I always thought that, if I could do something to make her life better and raise her standard of living, why shouldn't I? Material wealth helps to elevate and sustain levels of greatness and happiness. We can be positive enough to feel happy with what we currently have, but this does not mean that we can't have the desire to pursue better things. I was going to make it happen for my sister who had sacrificed her life for my family.

"Hey, congratulations! Your sister is going to get married. You must be so happy, since you have been worrying about it. Can I attend the wedding?" My friend's voice pulled me back to reality. The reality of the situation made me feel both pain and joy. I invited some close friends to the wedding, as I did before with my eldest sister's. Once again, this was to bring more love to my sister and help me cope with the torment I was going through.

My soul was lost all the way back to my hometown. I sat as silent as a stone.

"Hey, your phone has been ringing," my friend alerted me.

"Where have you guys been? Your sister is going crazy with worry. She got drunk and has been crying," a strange voice told me over the phone.

"Are you kidding me? My sister got drunk and cried? We will be home in around 15 minutes, we just had problems with our transportation. Please take care of her," I insisted, without asking who the guy on the phone was.

There was a flaring fire in my heart. I could not find a proper explanation in my mind for what I had heard on the phone.

"Are you ok? I have been worried about you. Why have you come home late? If you had had an accident, I would…" my sister said as she ran over to hug me, her eyes full of tears as I entered the gate.

"I'm sorry. You know that nothing could happen to me. You know your sister is really strong, and won't die that easily. You should have not cried today. Look at you, a beautiful bride crying on her wedding day," I tried to joke, as I had usually done.

I mentioned death casually, as I usually do in conversations with my sisters and parents. They would always stop me and insist that I shouldn't mention that word in such an innocent way.

"Don't say this again. I couldn't live if anything happened to you. You know that, don't you? Anyway, what do you want to eat? I will cook for you and your friends," my sister insisted.

My heart could not accommodate that immense love and generosity. I wanted to explode. This was the first time I had seen my sister getting drunk. She had never been drunk before, and never drank after. The question "What should I do?" came back again and snatched my heart, my soul. Shame, bitterness, hurt, suffering, and crying dominated my heart. It was the first time in my life I had wanted to run away from reality. I felt I was too small to deal with all the thoughts and suffering I was going through because of my sister's love for me. I felt like trying to run as fast as I could, but I could not; something held me back. I was totally trapped. I tried over and over again. I was still stuck.

I felt as if someone called me, saying: "Why do you want to run away? I am here." I looked back, to find my sister with the broken leg trying to catch me. In my imagination, I gently ran back and held my sister's hand to go back home together. I would never run away again, as I had her beside me.

My brother came in and hit me, suddenly awakening me from the flow of my imagination. I was at home, on my sister's wedding day. Instead of sinking into the daydream of blaming myself on my sister's happy day, it was better to take real, positive action to give her more happy days in the future.

In Vietnam, the occasion of marriage normally takes place over two days. The wedding consists of an extensive set of ceremonies: asking permission to receive the bride, receiving the bride at her house, and bringing the bride to the groom's house. The day of the groom coming and asking permission to receive the bride is usually the day of tears for the bride's parents and relatives. The tears of happiness to see the bride go to have her own happy life, worries about how everything will be going for her and sadness to not have her around everyday have become an emotional part of the wedding.

On that day, while taking pictures with my sister and her groom, all the feelings and questions came back again to my mind. I could not hold back my tears. I ran into a nearby field, and I screamed. I felt suffering and pain on my sister's happy day.

I was at the end of my tether, I blamed myself, not anyone else. I cried for the second time after I became aware of things around me. To my sister, having me was the greatest gift already. After crying like a child, I took a deep breath. **I knew that I had nothing else to do, but to turn any sad emotions on that wonderful day into real, positive actions. If I couldn't do it at that time, I would be motivated to make it happen one day.**

I went back to the wedding, and hugged my sister. I felt her empathy about what I had felt. I had no other words than those I spoke silently inside my heart, "Thank you, I love you, wait for me."

I was the reason
Some months after my sister's wedding, everyone talked about her baby. She became pregnant before her marriage with Truong, even though nobody had ever seen them go out of my family's house. The rumour, and whether it was true or not, didn't bother me as long as my sister was happy. I knew my sister well, and I thought it was probably not an accident.

I didn't ask her or anyone about it. All that I needed to know was that my sister was happy in her marriage.

I went back home one weekend. My sister was waiting for me at my parents' house, and she cooked favourite food for me, as always.

"I know it's not good for a girl to be pregnant before getting married, but I planned it," my sister told me while we were in the kitchen together.

"Who told you it isn't good? It's awesome as long as you are happy. Hold on - you said you planned it, so what was the plan exactly?"

"I wanted to have a baby who has the same zodiac sign as you, so we calculated the time to give birth this year. I want to have a wonderful baby to make me proud, just as you do."

"Wow, what a plan. So you want another dragon lady?"

"It can be a dragon boy, but still another wonderful dragon," she said with the most beautiful smile ever on her face.

"What should I do?" The question returned to my mind. I should be a good example for that upcoming dragon - the answer was obvious. It has been a MUST for me to be an inspirational aunt for the upcoming dragon.

In my entire life, I have never felt I needed my own child, since each child of my sisters and my brother has become mine. I feel I owe them love, care and everything, as I owed their mums and dad. My life should be to take care of them before I can take care of my own children.

My sister seems to be so sensitive about my gut feeling. She has never reminded me about getting married because she knows that I always want to remain a kid in her eyes and her kids are mine.

"I know you don't think about having a child or getting married. What about the feeling of creating a new life? A copy which is as wonderful as you are? This is the best feeling you can imagine."

"Wow, that's definitely a nice way to put it - really touching, sis. Although it's so nice, I can't take it, I am sorry. I have so many children now and upcoming children too. Look, your children, Tien's children, Lan's children. I don't need more."

Even though I spoke those words easily as usual, I felt touched inside. "Creating a new life, as wonderful as you are". Till now, if I ever think of getting married or having a baby, those words of my sister are the key motivation.

My sister doesn't read a lot, but she has experienced things that books are usually written about. She doesn't socialise a lot, but she has an honest heart, a heart of the most incredible person in society. She doesn't go around the world, but she is a world for me. She lets me into the world to see the courage, the desire, and everything that is a must in life. She lets me into the world to be non-stop living, loving and giving.

My HERO

One day in an imagination class I took part in at a social meeting, we did an exercise in which we closed our eyes and recalled an image that was stuck in our minds, and then relive the moment. The image of my brother and myself going fishing together came into my mind. The shadow of my brother was longer than mine, just like in the poem "The Sails" of Hoang Trung Thong.

A phone call pulled me back to the present. My brother called me, and I just smiled while talking to him because of the coincidence. Memories come back.

Everyone has an unforgettable image that sends them back to their childhood. Sometimes, we need to refresh our minds by getting back to old memories. The present is the moment, the little push that takes us far away from the childhood to have better memories. The connecting string never has an end, and if we do not continue stretching it, it will shrink back, and we will lose track.

If my eldest sister was my angel and spiritual leader, and my other elder sister was my Push to be the one I must be, my brother is my courageous hero to engage me to stay motivated and to keep fighting every moment of life. My brother has been a real Hero for me, ever since I was a small kid.

The first golden ticket
I was 3 years old.

It was a sunny afternoon, with the sun shining in every corner of our house. From the veranda of our house I could see the people working in the field through our garden. "You know the people in the field? Name them correctly and I will give you a surprise," my brother nodded his head and enticed me into guess, while carrying me and walking to the veranda.

My family's garden was huge, full of trees, and there were three tombs in the middle of it. A longan tree was located in the middle of the triangle of tombs to make it a perfect place for playing in the summer time. For most people, it would seem scary to live in a house with tombs, but for my family the tombs have become a part of our life. The shadow of the tree and the wind can make the tombs the best place to fall asleep just after a few minutes. For me and my siblings, it was a favourite place to play. The people buried in the three tombs had no relationship with my family. They died in the war and my grandfather buried them in our garden. Each year, their relatives would come to my family's house to pay tribute to them. They had tried to move the tombs to their hometown, but every time they tried to excavate them, some bad things would happen; a few people even died. In Vietnam, some suspicious people believe that excavating tombs can bring bad fortune, so it's better to leave them as they are. My family has considered the people buried in the tombs as our relatives. To me, the tombs are a fantastic place for sleeping and studying in the hot summer.

I named the people who were working in the field. My brother went away and then came back with a bottle full of colourful fish. "They are your little brothers. You will take care of them, won't you?" I had dreamt about raising fish before and my brother gave me a chance to make it happen. I saw amazing fish kept for enjoyment later in my life, but none of them could beat the ones my brother gave me. Simply, he taught me how to take care of a life. It was not easy to be a good brother.

That day my parents were in hospital taking care of my younger sister who passed away a few weeks after that. In the afternoon, my brother told me he would go to catch more beautiful fish for me so that I could agree to let him go. I stayed at home playing with my second sister who was 4 years older than me. We were playing on the SWING under the longan tree, near the three tombs. My sister would push me UP and I would laugh continuously as I sailed high into the air. Suddenly, the family dog barked, and a lady who was around 30 years old, with a bicycle, entered our house. My sister and I ran to the yard to talk to her.

"Hi, I am your mother's sister. Your parents want to see your sister and asked me to take her there," she told my elder sister, pointing at me.

My sister did not have enough time to figure out who the lady was, as she continued "And my bicycle was broken, so I have to take your family's bicycle to go there."

My sister had no idea how to respond, as the lady did not even let the 7-year-old kid have time to understand what was going on. She immediately grabbed the bicycle and prepared to leave. As I realised when I grew up, my family's bicycle at that time was really expensive and was our most valuable asset, as not many people in my village could afford to buy it. My father had run some business outside of his official work hours and saved money to buy it as a gift to my mother, so that she could use it to commute safely to the market every day.

She lifted me up onto the bicycle and rode away, leaving my sister behind bewildered.

I was behind her and did not have any idea either, as I just thought we were going to meet my parents, which, for me, was great since they had been away from home for almost a week. We went out of the house, and around 500 metres away, I suddenly I heard the voice of my brother. I looked back, he was panting after running a long distance, and he stopped the lady.

"I want to take my sister home. She isn't going anywhere. She is still too small to go to the hospital."

"But your parents want to see her," the lady insisted.

"My parents told us to take care of her at home. She will stay with us. You can go there alone. I have never seen you before" my brother said sternly.

"Ok".

The lady gave up arguing with my brother's determination, so she rode away as soon as she could. My brother held me tightly. I could feel his heart beating in his chest. I didn't know what had just happened, why my brother breathed rapidly, and why he ran as he took me back home. When I grew up, I came to realise the feeling my brother had, terrified, scared, confused, because the fact was that I was almost kidnapped. Unlike in normal kidnapping cases, the person who was horrified was my brother, while I felt happy as an innocent would-be kidnapped baby.

Nobody had any idea who the lady was, but everyone believed that she was a kidnapper. At that time in Vietnam, people kidnapped children to earn money. Some children in our province were kidnapped at that time. That was why there were some movies about children who were kidnapped and became successful in China, then went back to find their real parents. I grew up, and saw the relationship between reality and the trend in movies produced to talk about a mislaid girl who went back Vietnam to find her real parents. Whenever we talked about that experience, I would joke with my mum that I could have become a successful businesswoman abroad and come back to find them. My mum would always tell me it was the silliest idea she had heard of.

Deep within me, I would have never thought I'd be lucky enough to have that golden ticket to be myself in my wonderful family. My brother saved me. He gave me the golden ticket to be his sister, to be the daughter of my parents, and grow up in my amazing family for the rest of my life.

The second golden ticket
I was 5 years old.

It was a rainy day, like many others, when I followed my brother to go fishing. We ran on the grassy shore of the river covered in water. Suddenly, I found it difficult to breathe. I had stepped into a deep hole that was covered by unclean water. I was struggling with the water, trying to get out. I tried to call my brother, but the water was up to my mouth and started pouring inside my lungs and stomach. I heard his excited voice calling me to see the big fish, but I could not answer; I was about to stop breathing. A few minutes later, I was already on the ground, safe and sound, with my brother - who had a worried and terrified face - looking at me. He held me so tightly and took me home straight away. I was in his arms, and felt the same terrifying feeling he had when I was about to be the kidnapped.

My brother again saved me. He gave me the second golden ticket to be his sister, to be the daughter of my parents, and grow up in my amazing family for the rest of my life.

My brother-made childhood

Summer time

Whenever the rainy season came, I would be excited to go fishing with my brother. The drowning incident did not scare me as long as my brother was with me. With shorts and a boy's cap, I was ready to follow my brother to fish with a bamboo pot. The bamboo pot is a half of an oval shape with a handle in the middle to make it easy to carry and place in the water to round up the fish into the pot. My brother was called a fish hunter as he knew where exactly he could catch a lot of fish. We were such a great team; it never took us more than an hour to fill the whole basket, 40cm long and 30cm wide. My brother saw it in my eyes that I very much wanted to be the fisher rather than the carrier, so he arranged for me to fish in a place with a lot of fish to cheer me up sometimes, or to trap me into a place without fish to disappoint me so that I would then let him get on with his job.

The drowning incident also made my brother keep me away from places with deep water as much as possible. He would even lift me over small puddles. When I was 10 years old, 15 or even 23, he would still do the same thing with me. I feel safe and protected every time I'm with him. He is my hero.

"You will fly as high as the kite, but remember the string to keep you up is our family," my brother whispered into my ears, as he taught me how to control the kite in the sky.

My mischievous trainer left me when I was 11 years old and went to Ho Chi Minh City (in the Soul of Vietnam, our family is in the North) to make a living and pursue further education. I became a fish killer in the village.

My brother taught me how to be a good hunter - to be able to live in the current environment, the current society, and the current world.

Autumn time

When the autumn came, I would be ready to go to trap birds in the field with my brother. I would take the bag and follow my brother to the field, set up the trap and come back home.

In the afternoon, we would go back to the field to collect all the trapped birds. We would take pine tar pitch and put it on the ground with some bait. My crisp laugh whenever I saw trapped birds became a motivation for my brother to trap more birds.

To be a brother is sometimes so difficult, but in the meantime brings a feeling of happiness. That was what I got from my brother. It seemed to be easy to be a naughty sister, and the happy feeling is the best.

My brother taught me how to be happy by making others happy.

Spring time

When the spring came, I would be excited to go to play spinning top with my brother. My brother taught me how to make good spinning tops from wood. I would go to play with the other boys and always be so proud, thanks to the well-designed top. It was easy for me to beat the other boys, but it was hard to beat my brother, except for when he pretended to be a loser. He would always encourage me, saying each time I lost to him that I could win the next time. "Start over. You'll win the next round. You're my courageous sister who will never give up."

My brother taught me how to compete and to work in a team. My brother taught me how to never give up.

Winter time

When the winter came, I would be ready to go to the field to fry sweet potato with my brother. We, together with other kids, also took the buffalo to the field. After the harvest, the field was empty, so together we would put the sweet potato on the fire. My brother taught me how to ride the buffalo and take control of the situation. It was terrifying the first time; I ran away from the buffalo and he chased me. I screamed and cried and called my brother's name. My brother stopped the buffalo just with a strong determined voice. I wondered how he could do that; he just smiled and told me to domesticate the buffalo and show it that my intention is to be friends with it. He took my hand and put it on the horn of the buffalo, and I brushed its hair and looked in its eyes. I became a great friend of the buffalo afterwards and would race with my brother on the buffalo's back.

My brother taught me how to take control of the situation in a wild environment, in society and in the world.

Good times do not last forever, bad times likewise, but we can always have a better time. Nobody can be beside us every day in our entire life; people come and go. The most important thing is that we need to have the courage to stand on our own feet as people will always be there in our heart, despite the time, despite the space. I tried to come to terms with my brother's departure from our hometown to stand on his own feet in the south of Vietnam at the age of 18.

My brother-made adulthood

First route chosen

He was 18 years old. He was a young, good-looking man. Some people compared him to a Korean super star since he had a strong white skin, bright eyes and a muscled body.

No matter how hard my parents tried to stop my brother from applying to one of the most difficult universities in Vietnam, even the wrong set of subjects, he did anyway. He made the decision for his own future, he told me: "Your brother either does not take the exam or takes the most difficult one."

He was an intelligent boy and determined enough to decide what he thought he wanted to do. He did not pass the exam, as everyone expected. Most importantly, he did not pass the exam because of his carefully designed plan. He told my parents that he wanted to work in an electronic shop in the city to gain more experience and earn money while preparing for the next year's university exam. The decision was out of my parents' hands, so they just let him do it – he would have done it anyway, whatever their opinion.

Half a year later, my brother left our hometown to go to the south with the aim of challenging himself and making a living, and at the same time pursuing his further education. This was again out of my parents' hands; it was something that they had to let happen.

My brother chose his own path to step forwards.

Risky route given

"Hey, get out." Everyone was shouting this outside of the restaurant engulfed in flames, I imagined. "Is there anyone inside?" "No, the restaurant was closed, so there should be nobody inside."

A young man, burnt, walked out of the burning building. It was my brother.

The image of the building on fire was in front of my eyes and on my mind. I imagined all this as soon as I heard about my brother's accident. My brother walked out of the burnt building as Hero Hesman.

That year my brother came home for the Chinese New Year by motorbike. He travelled all the way from the South to the North alone; he came home with a sun-burnt face. "I lost all the books and all things I bought for you. They were burnt. Only this is left," he said, as he gave me a small Hero Hesman toy.

"How could you not get burnt then? You should have jumped inside to try to save all the things, as heroes do in movies," I joked innocently.

"I would have done that if I knew you were dying to have those things more than your brother," he laughed.

"I would then jump in to save you as Hero Hesman, and get you and those things out," I laughed in an even louder voice than my brother's.

I knew the truth was that my brother had almost died because of that fire incident. As I heard from my parents, my brother was trusted enough by the owners of the restaurant so they let him manage the whole restaurant. He was sleeping on the second floor, and only woke up when he found it difficult to breathe. The smoke filled the whole building, my brother was lucky to get out of the restaurant and to be alive.

Life put my Hero onto a risky route, but his courage and his desire to live brought him back to his chosen path. It did not scare him, but made him stronger. Death did not scare him, so nothing else could. My Hero is not afraid of anything, so neither am I.

My brother-made student life
"Are you coming home this week?"

"Maybe not. You know I get sick of the bus, unless you come and pick me up. Hahahaha."

"Ok".

My brother chuckled. I hung up and continued my work, with the understanding that he acknowledged the fact that I would not go back to my hometown that time.

"Hi, I am in front of your hostel now. Prepare and come down to go home," my brother said to me on the phone 2 hours later.

"You must be kidding. I will try and come home next week," I laughed excitedly. "Go out and look down and you can see me. You told me to pick you up, didn't you?" he told me casually, as if it was an obvious thing. "Yes, but". I do not like using the word BUT when talking to people, since I consider it as an excuse, as my brother does. I shut up and went outside.

"I am crazy, but I would be never as crazy as he is, if he really came around", I said this to myself while running outside. I saw my brother with the motorbike waiting for me. He had just driven all the way down from my hometown over 70km away to pick me up because I said so, even though he told me he was at a meeting in his office. I was surprised enough, but not shocked, given his history. He wouldn't mind driving his motorbike for 200km every week to see a girl, and he had done it for five years. Later in my life, I did a similar thing; I would cross the border of the country to see a guy I liked after two weeks of working with him. I would cross the continent to see a guy I admired after two hours of talking.

"Where is Tien, is he there with you?" my sister hurriedly asked me on the phone. "Oh yes, I just saw he arrived here. Amazing, isn't it?" I tried to calm her down, as usual.

My eldest sister is the most thoughtful person I have ever known in my entire life. She takes care of everyone; she knows where everyone goes and what everyone wants. She knew exactly when he left to come to my place and she was worried about him going by motorbike. In Vietnam, travelling by motorbike on the highway for a long distance is not the ideal way to travel. We have witnessed different serious accidents on the highway with motorbikes; my sister would never want to see it happen to anyone around her.

"He is a strong man. We'll be careful," I talked innocently again.

"I'm not kidding; he shouldn't have done that. You shouldn't have told him to do it," she got more serious.

"OK. I actually didn't intend to, but it's cool when it happens for real. I think we'll repeat it. We won't let you be worried. I'm going to prepare to go home now. See you soon. I know you want to see me, love you," I provoked my sister.

As a naughty girl, I tried to reassure my sister so as to finish the call as soon as possible to avoid hearing her complaint again. I picked up some gifts I had got for my family and took my bag and ran to my brother.

As I said to my sister, afterwards my brother would pick me up every time he felt I was too lazy to go home. He seemed to be the man in my life, strong, determined, and sensitive. He took action to express his love. He didn't use words. We didn't use words. We had a special connection. I looked back at my whole life and saw we crossed similar paths together. On each path, we had the same hungry foolishness and we kept going forward. He is my Hero Hesman.

I knew that I could not stop him doing things for me even though it might be dangerous. I knew one thing I could do for him which was to stay strong, to feel blessed and pay it back by living courageously. I knew I could do one thing for him which was to find the hero within myself. I knew I could do one thing for him which was to be a hero for someone else as he has been for me.

My-made brother girlfriend

When it comes to romantic love, people think that the loved one would become more important than anyone else. In the case of my brother, the loved one needed to be with my family, needed to love my family, needed to have special feelings towards everyone in the family. Most importantly, the loved one needed to love me and be loved by me.

"Hey, I want you to talk to a girl. You can use yahoo," my brother demanded.

"Did you mean a boy? Why do I need to talk to a girl?" I joked, and started to feel he was going to introduce someone really important to him to the sister he loved most.

"No, it is she. She is important to me," he nodded.

"Even more than me?" I just talked nonsense to provoke my brother so that he had to tell me she was his girlfriend.

"I will text you her Yahoo account in a few minutes' time, check it out and talk to her when you have time."

"So, what can I get after that, my commander?" I laughed.

"Remember to check it, I will hang up", my brother said.

I became close to the girl in some ways, and I knew she was not his girlfriend but more important than that. My brother had loved her for five years, even though she had a boyfriend. My brother loved the girl unconditionally and maturely. He would visit her every week and spend time with her as a good friend. He did not have a blind love. He was just a person who got a true love feeling for the first time in his life, so he just wanted to love completely and make an effort to get it.

He taught me how to love completely.

He finally achieved a stable presence in our hometown. As a Hero, he went back to our hometown to take responsibility as a man in the family as my parents got older.

New Hesman

Bright eyes, intellectual face, ready anytime to go to save the world - I saw all this in his little son, my little hero, my nephew. My Hero brought another Hero to the world.

The story of Hesman details the adventure of an intelligent and partially autonomous robot and its human companions. Hesman and the team travel the Galaxy, fighting against various antagonists to defend the peace of universe.

My Hesman travelled around to find himself, to win the hearts of all people he met and to be able to help people to stay as courageous as Heroes. My Hesman created a Hero within myself, for real.

What is the thing you feel most thankful for in life?
One day, in a public speaking club, I was randomly given a question "What is the thing you feel most thankful for in life?" I had no hesitation to say "To be alive". We only feel that when we almost take the opportunity to continue living. Seeing my sister's and my brother's sacrifices and losses, I always feel that I have been lucky to be alive. Seeing how amazingly my brother and sisters overcome difficulties, I always feel confident to do whatever it takes. As long as I am alive, I can, non-stop, be loving, giving and making a difference for myself, my family and people around me.

People have asked me where my infinite love comes from, where my infinite energy comes from, how it has been maintained, how it increases moment after moment, day after day, how it has helped me live meaningfully, positively and purposefully and how I could, non-stop, be living, loving and giving. This book is my thankful answer.

Be it windy, sunny, foggy, freezing or stormy, there is always a smiley yellow kite flying in the sky. The kite has become a part of people's lives. People believe the kite was made by a beautiful angel, with a must-be strong string and flown by a Hero flyer. People have no hesitation but create their own kites.

This is your time. Today is the day to be non-stop living, loving and giving to achieve more!

Talk soon!

_jenvuhuong.com

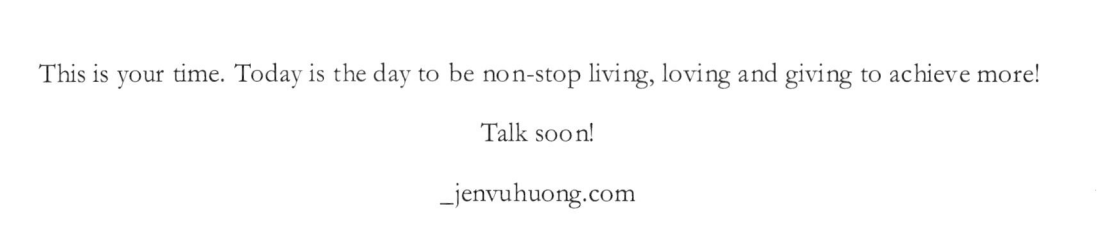

How is Jen now?

Keep updated Jen's books in the nonstop loving, living, and giving series at jenvuhuong.com/books

Gratitude moments

I have felt deeply grateful for life's golden tickets given by my sisters and my brother. I live each day to earn that blessing, and in my efforts to be non-stop living, loving and giving.

This book is dedicated to my sisters, my brother.

My eldest sister Lan has a lovely family. She has two kids, a boy and a girl. She lives in a good living condition with her kind husband. She has been promoted in her job, as her husband has. She goes to work every day, and she passes by my family every day after finishing work. She texts me every day. She smiles every time she hears my voice. She feels happy every time she thinks about how her sister is trying to become the person she wants to be, to make her proud of her.

My other elder sister Toi also has a lovely family. She has a boy. She is going to have another child soon. She is happier than anyone else, not because she has a fancy job, but just simply because she loves it, she loves working as a seller in the market. Her husband got a well-paid job, and their standard of living has improved day by day. She wakes up early to go to the market every day, and prepares food for my parents every day after finishing work. She texts me once or twice a week. She smiles every time she thinks about how her younger sister is trying to become the person she must be, to make all the best things happen for her.

My elder brother, Tien, also has a lovely family. He has a boy. He works for the government. He is loved by people whenever he organises a charity event. He goes to work every day. He goes to fish as a hobby sometimes. He smiles when fishing and thinking about fishing memories with me. He calls me once or twice a month. He smiles every time he thinks about how his younger sister is trying her best to find a hero inside herself to make a difference to her family, to the people around her, and to herself.

My parents are not worried as before, and are happier more than ever to be surrounded by all their grandchildren. They still work every day. They sometimes call me. They smile when they think about their small child who has a huge burning desire to live for her family, and for the people around her.

Myself, I wake up every morning grateful that I am alive, with the vibrancy of non-stop living, loving and giving. Despite the distance and time, my heart is always with my family. With my family - my faith, my angel, my must and my hero, the kite has no other choice but to be together with the people around it happy, non-stop living, loving and giving their best.

To the Editor M. Ibrahim and my friend Sophie who helped me edit the book. Without you, the publishing book journey would have not been going well.

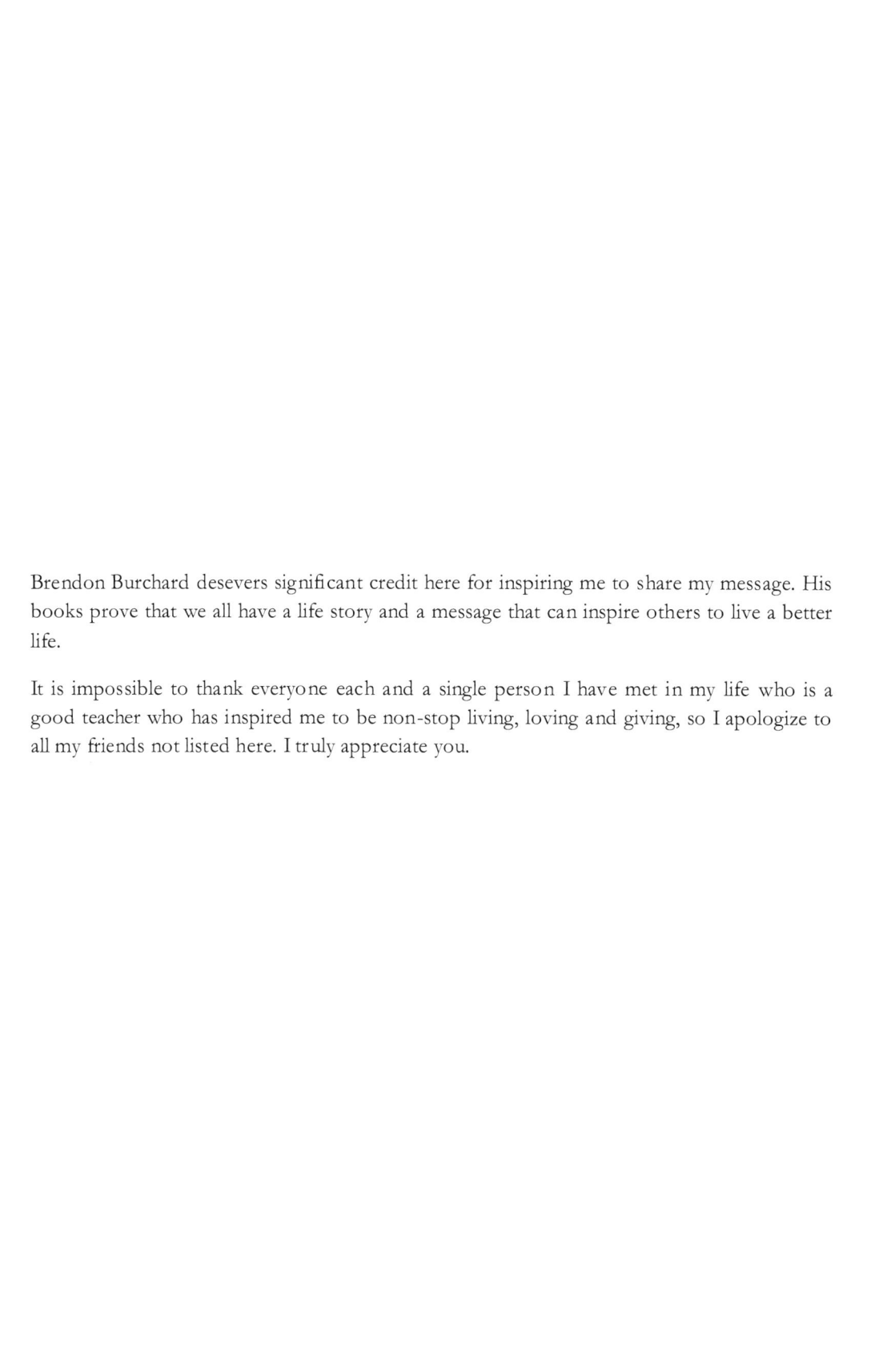

Brendon Burchard desevers significant credit here for inspiring me to share my message. His books prove that we all have a life story and a message that can inspire others to live a better life.

It is impossible to thank everyone each and a single person I have met in my life who is a good teacher who has inspired me to be non-stop living, loving and giving, so I apologize to all my friends not listed here. I truly appreciate you.

About the Author

Jen Vuhuong (Full Vietnamese name: Vu Thi Huong) graduated from Hanoi University of Science and Technology in Electronics and Telecommunications. She was awarded a scholarship by Samsung Corporation in her final year at university, where she worked for two years. She then completed her master's in Business Innovation and Technology Management in Europe with a full Erasmus scholarship. Later, she moved to work in Malaysia for a Dell partner for almost two years. Apart from her engineering job, she has worked as an event organiser and MC in various English clubs, social networks and public speaking communities in Asia as well as in Europe. She devoted five months to working as an event organiser for a campaign of a Belgian NGO before studying a master's in International Management in the UK with a Chevening (British Government) scholarship.

After engaging in personal and social development since 2011, Jen has started pursue her career as a personal development trainer, speaker, writer, coach, consultant to empower people to reach their potential to make a difference in life. She particularly focuses on high performance, leadership, and career development areas.

Jen is thankful to have been given different opportunities to continue living, to have been loved unconditionally and to have been given all the best things. She has been amazed by every single person she has met who has lived fully, loved completely and given devotedly. She has been inspired to be non-stop living, loving and giving every moment of her life and as a duty to inspire people around her to do so.

Meet Jen, join her performance/leadership community, coaching programmes, courses, and books and her weekly inspiring videos at the website: **jenvuhuong.com** or connect Jen via jenvuhuong@gmail.com

Let's be nonstop loving, living, giving every moment of life.

Printed in Great Britain
by Amazon